a pocketful of
RHYME

Imagination for a new generation

2006 Poetry Competition for 7-11 year-olds

Young Writers

Nottinghamshire

Edited by Lynsey Hawkins

Young Writers

First published in Great Britain in 2007 by:
Young Writers
Remus House
Coltsfoot Drive
Peterborough
PE2 9JX
Telephone: 01733 890066
Website: www.youngwriters.co.uk

SB ISBN 1 84602 728 4

Foreword

Young Writers was established in 1991 and has been passionately devoted to the promotion of reading and writing in children and young adults ever since. The quest continues today. Young Writers remains as committed to the nurturing of poetic and literary talent as ever.

This year's Young Writers competition has proven as vibrant and dynamic as ever and we are delighted to present a showcase of the best poetry from across the UK and in some cases overseas. Each poem has been selected from a wealth of *A Pocketful Of Rhyme* entries before ultimately being published in this, our fourteenth primary school poetry series.

Once again, we have been supremely impressed by the overall quality of the entries we have received. The imagination, energy and creativity which has gone into each young writer's entry made choosing the poems a challenging and often difficult but ultimately hugely rewarding task - the general high standard of the work submitted ensured this opportunity to bring their poetry to a larger appreciative audience.

We sincerely hope you are pleased with this final collection and that you will enjoy *A Pocketful Of Rhyme Nottinghamshire* for many years to come.

Contents

Charlotte Allsopp (8)	77
Emily Cooper (8)	78
Demi Stanley (10)	79
Josh Mansell (10)	80
Charlotte Hart (8)	81
Aimee Flear (8)	82
Jack Eaton (9)	83
Oliver Cooper-Bannister (10)	84
Curtis Atkinson (10)	85
Reanne Broomfield (10)	86
Sean Revill (10)	87
Amber Caudwell (9)	88
Lauren Moles (8)	89
Jordan Cowen (8)	90
Isobel Davis (9)	91
George Loaring (8)	92
Chayse Hayes (8)	93
Liam King (9)	94
Bethany Durham (8)	95
Rebecca Glasier (10)	96
Jordan Wright (9)	97
Samuel Bacon (8)	98
Elizabeth Fidler (8)	99
Adam Flear (10)	100
Aaron Bradley (10)	101
James Hudson (10)	102
Laura Murray (10)	103
Leon Savastio-Birkbeck (10)	104
Olivia Zeraati (10)	105
Tamara Cartwright (10)	106
Ellie Hatt (10)	107
Matt Tunnard (10)	108
Lauren Hotson (11)	109
Lauren Tong (10)	110
Katie O'Sullivan (10)	111
Joseph Murphy (10)	112
Iago Thomas (9)	113
Katy Adams (9)	114
Jamie Jenkins (9)	115
Becki Partridge (9)	116
Jasmine Cross (9)	117
Emily Rewston (9)	118

Jessica Speirs (10)	119
Mitchell Gleaden (9)	120
Danielle Hammond (10)	121
Daniel Moody (10)	122
Kristien Gregory (9)	123
James Bacon (9)	124
Ryan Spires (10)	125
Jakob Higson (10)	126
Richard Caldwell (10)	127
Rhiannon Smith (11)	128

Middleton Primary School

Nicole Patara (8)	129
Amin Ahmadi (8)	130
Isabel Prince (8)	131
John Mikhail (8)	132
Georgia Sheridan-Parker (7)	133
Aston Morgan (8)	134
Inshaal Akbar (8)	135
Aimee Clay (7)	136
Joshua Stables (8)	137
Amelia Lewin (7)	138
Junaid Aslam (8)	139
Gemma Pearson (7)	140
Robyn Atkinson (7)	141
Damon Wright (8)	142
Naomi Squire (8)	143
Husnain Rasool (7)	144
Katherine Griffin-Pearce (7)	145
Rebecca Griffin-Pearce (7)	146
William Russell-Fishwick (9)	147
Emily Kirk (8)	148
Lauren Hammond (8)	149
Darnell Nugent (7)	150
Sena Mamurekli (8)	151
Tamara Falcone (7)	152
Morgan Wills (8)	153
Abigail Ensor (7)	154
Alina Akhter (8)	155
George Burton (8)	156
Laura Smedley (7)	157

Ayesha Azad (8)   158
Nicky Kirkwood (8)   159
Scott Skerritt (8)   160
Simran Trevett-Singh (7)   161
Libby Scutts (8)   162
Ben Upjohn (8)   163
Molly Round (7)   164
Rahuldeep Bawa (8)   165
Sumeyye Esil (8)   166
Samerah Iqbal (8)   167
Alice Porter (7)   168
Ishrat Hussain (7)   169
Alex Chamberlain (7)   170
Tamika Gayle (8)   171
Lucy Bradley (7)   172
Hamza Tahir (8)   173
Phabian Graham (7)   174
Mollie Newth (8)   175
Sophia Dryden (7)   176
Emma Hinnells (8)   177
Callum Brown (8)   178
Alice Mai Sheridan-Parker (7)   179
Ibraheem Belim (8)   180
Olivia Rose Janmaat (7)   181
Jack Mee (8)   182
Shayna McPherson (7)   183
Daniel Andrew (8)   184
Thomas Judson (7)   185

St Peter's CE Primary School, East Bridgford
Amy Ashmore (10)   186
Luchia Ecott (10)   187
Lorna Rose Douglas (10)   188
Emma Hopewell-Ward (10)   189
Alexandra Chick (11)   190
Daniel Thurman (10)   191
Daniel Hayes (10)   192
Matthew Sutton (10)   193
Hannah Jayne Parker (10)   194
Jessica Morrell (10)   195
Brittany Howe (10)   196

The Poems

Fireworks In The Air

Rushing
Orange sparks
Catherine wheels
Taking off from the ground
Everyone watching
Toffee apples.

Hana Hussain (7)

Hallowe'en

Hallowe'en is near
It will surely give you a scare

Witches soaring through the moonlit sky
Skeletons clatter towards you and say, 'Trick or treat!'

Pumpkins shimmering golden rays!
Children collecting sweets to eat.

Dracula sucking blood,
Zombies stomping down the road like a herd of elephants.
Witches laughing.
Happy Hallowe'en.

Joshua Quail (10)
Brocklewood Junior School

Hallowe'en Is Near

Hallowe'en is near
It might give you a scare!

The pumpkin's eyes light up the dark,
Like the sun on the horizon.

The spooky spiders speak so slyly
That the houses shake and tremble.

As Dracula sucks your blood, the witches fly on their brooms
As deadly zombies walk towards you.

Daniel King (10)
Brocklewood Junior School

Winter

On a winter's night and the sky is dull,
Not a soul on Earth feels complete or full.

Everywhere covered in snow, water and ice,
Kids stay in and play board games with dice.

Everyone bored and lonely they are
Here, there, near and far.

Dark, cold and miserable is the night,
Kids playing board games then argue and fight.

Alex Shawcroft (10)
Brocklewood Junior School

Brocklewood Teachers

Mr Grain is really funny
I think he has a fluffy bunny.

Mrs Carey has a lovely smile
She talks to us about the Nile.

Mrs Hobdell she makes lovely cakes
At the weekend she sits by lakes.

Mrs Taylor Smith is new to the school
When you get to know her she is cool.

Mrs Shipley teaches literacy
Her favourite book is 'Nitracy'.

Miss Wiser went and then came back
She climbed a mountain with a backpack.

Miss Sharp is off poorly-sick
I hope she comes back really quick.

Miss Gamston teaches history
She likes to solve a mystery.

Miss Tarrant is having a baby
If it's a girl she can call her Maisy.

The other staff work so hard
And play with me in the yard.

At last Miss Hart, who really hates mud!
I'm proud to be at Brocklewood.

Victoria Harris (8)
Brocklewood Junior School

No It Doesn't Match

Bill said red matches with blue
I said red matches with pink
Bill said as red as a rose
I said as red as a bug.

Luke said as green as the grass
I said green is the best
Luke said green is blue
I said as green as gold.

Bradley said pink is for aliens
I said pink is for girls
Bradley said pink is for dresses
I said pink goes with yellow.

Lee said gold is for fools
I said gold is for pools
Lee said gold is so cool
I said gold makes you rich!

Luke Batchelor (9)
Brocklewood Junior School

School

School is cool,
You can play on computers,
You can read,
You can write,
You can have parties,
You can play with your mates,
You can have drink and biscuits,
You can have golden time,
You can draw,
You can colour,
You can put your hand up,
You can play,
You can learn,
You can celebrate,
You can enjoy.

Sophie Shilton-Lawlor (9)
Brocklewood Junior School

Monster

A monster ran past our classroom window,
It moved like a comet zooming through the sky.
His head the size of a hot ball of fire,
His ears the shape of a pointed tower,
His horns as sharp as a bright silver dagger,
Skin of a rubber tyre on a car,
Big, yellow, shiny marble eyes,
His paws like elephants stomping around,
His claws were silver, like a long, sharp sword,
He was as tall as a beanstalk,
His nose, the size of a bull's foot,
Listening to the children in the classroom working
Sniffing the air for food or foe,
No one else saw him,
No one looked up from their books,
Everyone a zombie.
I hope he comes back tomorrow.

Ashley Edwards (9)
Brocklewood Junior School

Autumn

Autumn leaves are falling down
Red, yellow and golden-brown
Swirling, hailing to the ground
Sleeping safely on the ground.

Worthwhile Breeze Sibanda (9)
Brocklewood Junior School

The Giant Thing

A thing, like a giant, ran past our classroom.
It moved as fast as a motorbike in a race.
His tail was a club of spikes.
His ears were balls of fire.
Mini crystals were his eyes.
Giant, black, dull brown paws.
His skin was like a rocky mountain.
He was as tall as a lamp post.
His nose was like a blazing red ruby.
Sniffing the air for food or foe.

No one else saw him
No one looked up from their work.
Everyone, a zombie.

Dylan Wallace (9)
Brocklewood Junior School

The Creature

A creature ran past our classroom window.
It moved as sly as a fox.
His tail was like a mace prepared to hit you.
His ears were like sharks' teeth.
His claws were like thorns.
He had blood-red eyes.
He had paws like a mammoth
His horns were as sharp as daggers
His skin was as spiky as a hedgehog
He was as tall as the heavens
He had a rabbit's nose
Sniffing the air for food or foe

No one else saw him
No one looked up from their books
Everyone a zombie
I hope he comes back tomorrow.

Ingrid McLaren (9)
Brocklewood Junior School

Hallowe'en

Hallowe'en is very spooky,
Children dressing up like witches
And zombies.

Pumpkins flickering their eyes
In the sparkling moonlight.

Children banging on doors,
Saying trick or treat
To old ladies
And men!

Witches are black bin bags
On their broomsticks.

Scary, spooks, scaring people stupid.

Leah Hartley-Dames (11)
Brocklewood Junior School

Hallowe'en

Manky zombies come from the cracked floors
Hands grabbing from different coloured doors
Zombies standing proudly like statues waiting
For their prey to pass in the baby-blue sea water

Zombies that are werewolves howling in the silver moonlight
Zombies smiling evilly under the red fiery clouds
Zombies like the Devil casting a spell in the dark, evil world
Zombies rising from the dead ground.

Ryan Allen (10)
Brocklewood Junior School

Winter

The snowman is
standing proudly,
Waiting for the children to
destroy him.

Across the roads,
The trees are covered
with snow.

The children are playing,
Playing happily,
It's winter.

The white snow
is as white as the sheep.

The white snow melts
just like an ice cream,
Getting ready for summer.

Faith Thondolo (10)
Brocklewood Junior School

Hallowe'en

Hallowe'en is full of spooks.
Hallowe'en is where pumpkins' eyes flicker.
Hallowe'en is full of people dressing up.
Hallowe'en is when people trick or treat.
Hallowe'en is like somebody scaring you!

Witches, goblins and ghosts come out at night
Scaring everybody around them,
Ghosts are cloth knocking on doors.
Wicked witches flying around on wiry wood.
Decorative pumpkins scare people as they stroll past the window.
Children scaring people as they run past them.
We love Hallowe'en!

Aimie Mills (10)
Brocklewood Junior School

Hallowe'en

Hallowe'en is full of spooks
Things that jump and make you puke.
Hallowe'en costumes make you jump.
Pumpkins as orange as a goldfish.

Pumpkins sit still like a zombie.
Little children scaring you out of your wits.
Pumpkins pointing in the dark.
Ghouly ghost gasping for breath.
Mummies are a big ball of tissue.

Leanne Bradshaw (10)
Brocklewood Junior School

I Want To Paint

I want to paint a shining magical rose shimmering in the sunlight.
I want to paint a magical growing shimmering sunflower.
I want to paint a cute, ugly, snuffling pig.
I want to paint some tickly grass on my toes.
I want to paint a violet a gorgeous violet.
I want to paint a splodge of staining ink.

Amy White (7)
Carr Hill Primary School

I Want To Paint

I want to paint a red, flaming, pointy, hot fire.
I want to paint a yellow sunflower with a thin starry sunflower
and huge pointy petals.
I want to paint a pink pig with its chubby curled tail
with a big golden ring in its nose.
I want to paint green grass long, tickling, dark grass.
I want to paint an orange juicy holed orange.
I want to paint a purple plum which looks like a lovely ripe plum.
I want to paint a blue sea wavy, salty, bright sea.

Ronan Tunnard (7)
Carr Hill Primary School

The Blitz

The war is here
It's all clear.
But not for long
The Germans are strong
But we will win
And bring
Happiness to Britain.

The Blitz came
What a shame, what a shame
Will I survive or will I die?

Martin Hunt (8)
Carr Hill Primary School

Seasons

Winter
It's cold and bare
No one's out, it's icy
Blistering snow falls from the sky
It's wet.

Summer
It's really hot
People are sunbathing
Children are playing on the streets
It's hot.

Autumn
Leaves are falling
They are scattered all over
You can hear the leaves crunching
Autumn

It's spring
Flowers are here
Everyone is outside
You can see the growth of the plants
Spring, spring

Paige Thompson (10)
Carr Hill Primary School

Feelings

As happy as . . .
As happy as a baby's first smile
As happy as waking up on Christmas morning
As happy as the birds singing in the morning.

As sad as . . .
As sad as a relative dying
As sad as no friends to play with
As sad as your pet dying.

As surprised as saving a penalty in the World Cup final
As surprised as seeing an old friend who you haven't see in ages
As surprised as your baby brother's first word.

Darcey Vardy (10)
Carr Hill Primary School

I Want To Paint

I want to paint a red-hot flamy fire.
I want to paint a yellow big ball of fire.
I want to paint a pink chubby pink pig with a curly tail.
I want to paint some straight pointy bits of green grass.
I want to paint a tangy, juicy, round, yummy orange.
I want to paint a purple, tiny, round, shiny plum.
I want to paint a cloudless bright blue sky with beautiful birds.

Ryan Tate (7)
Carr Hill Primary School

I Want To Paint

I want to paint a juicy, sour apple, hard and crunchy.
I want to paint a fiery red and yellow heat.
I want to paint a big fat pig sitting in the mud.
I want to paint a green football pitch ready to play on.
I want to paint a big sour and juicy orange.
I want to paint a purple plum hanging in a tree.
I want to paint a blue sea crashing on the rocks.

Thomas Swannack (8)
Carr Hill Primary School

I Want To Paint

I want to paint a red rose, a bright beautiful rose.
I want to paint a yellow banana, a squidgy smooth banana.
I want to paint a pink pig, a smelly muddy pig.
I want to paint green grass, spiky prickly grass.
I want to paint an orange, a round, sweet, sour orange.
I want to paint purple lavender, tall lovely lavender.
I want to paint a blue sea, a wavy transparent sea.

Alia Issa (7)
Carr Hill Primary School

Evacuation

I'm waiting for the train
It is a pain,
Will I ever see my dad again?
The train's whistle loudly peeps,
I wish I could get some sleep.
What I saw was great,
Some cows, some sheep locked up in a gate.
When I got off the train
I messed with the windowpane.
I evacuated to a little house
Which had some rats and a mouse.
The owner ironed my clothes without a crease
And folded them very neat.

Brady Joe Lancaster (9) & Ellis Chambers (8)
Carr Hill Primary School

The Blitz Poem

I heard a rumble in the night.
I looked out of the window and it was very bright.
There were a few planes bombing the sky,
And fire getting very high.
The sound of houses crumbling down,
Then it made an awful sound.
I hope no bombs drop on me.

Curtis Pearce (9) & Lydia Davies (8)
Carr Hill Primary School

The Blitz Poem

Siren sounds overhead
Planes are coming on their way
We would like to drift away
Until these bombs stop.
Mum said, 'We will win this war of greed
And then it will be over indeed.'
After the war everybody
Will be able to run wild
Like they did before.

Courtney L Whitehead (8)
Carr Hill Primary School

The Evacuation Poem

As I left my mum,
I sang a song,
When I looked out of the window,
In the sunlight I saw cows,
Munching chewy grass
On the fields.
While watching this,
I was chomping on bread buns and biscuits,
And had a glass of orange juice,
It was a lovely sight,
Then in the distance I saw a white cotton ball,
It was a fluffy sheep,
Then finally I got off the train,
My foster parents were really nice,
Then I had a glass of juice with ice.

Meike Tomlinson & Aaron Campbell (8)
Carr Hill Primary School

The Evacuation

I was sitting in the train in the rain.
I looked out of the window
And saw some flowers growing
In the sun whilst eating my biscuits.
I was feeling so very happy
Then I arrived in a little cottage.
I felt sad because I missed my mum and dad,
My new family said, 'You will see them soon.'

Ruby Legge (9)
Carr Hill Primary School

Evacuation Poem

I am missing Mum and Dad
And I am so sad.
I hope I have got my gas mask
Or I might breathe my last.
And I want the train to be fast
I hope my house won't get blown up
I hope my dad has good luck fighting in World War II.
The train has arrived now, I feel fine.
And I don't want Dad to slip on the mine.

Nina Westerman (8)
Carr Hill Primary School

The Blitz

The war is here,
It's all clear,
But not for long,
For the Germans are strong,
But we will win,
And bring happiness to Britain.

The Blitz has come,
What a shame,
What a shame,
Will I survive
Or will I die?

Philip Wilson (8)
Carr Hill Primary School

I Want To Paint

I want to paint a yellow yolk, a dribbly runny yolk.
I want to paint a pink bobble, a big leather bobble.
I want to paint a green swamp, a gooey, bubbly, ugly swamp.
I want to paint orange juice, a cold sweet liquid running
                                            down my throat.
I want to paint purple ink, a dark liquid splashing on the paper.
I want to paint a blue sea, a deep dark substance where
                                            creatures live.

Tristan Briers (7)
Carr Hill Primary School

I Want To Paint

I want to paint lava, very hot and flaming.
I want to paint a sunflower, colourful and petally.
I want to paint a glittery bobble, a diamond bobble.
I want to paint grass, spiky and muddy.
I want to paint an orange, very sour and very sweet.
I want to paint a pansy, soft and beautiful.
A bluebell is very blue and gorgeous.

Jonathan Wood (7)
Carr Hill Primary School

I Want To Paint

I want to paint a red rose, a smooth, shining, bright rose.
I want to paint a yellow lemon, a strong, sour, juicy lemon.
I want to paint pink ice cream, creamy, swirly, pink ice cream.
I want to paint the prickly muddy grass.
I want to paint a juicy-smelling orange.
I want to paint purple lavender, the tall, beautiful, lovely lavender.
I want to paint blue sea, the shimmering, waving blue sea.

Lucy Shannon (8)
Carr Hill Primary School

I Want To Paint . . .

I want to paint . . . a bright phone box standing in the distance.
I want to paint . . . some squishy squeezy sweetcorn melting
                                                in my mouth.
I want to paint . . . a fluttering fairy flying in the sky.
I want to paint . . . some long grass shimmering in the sunlight.
I want to paint . . . a slow sideways crab crunching through the sand.
I want to paint . . . some crunchy beetroot bunched up in a bowl.
I want to paint . . . a Carr Hill T-shirt blue on my soft skin.

Sophie Lazenby (7)
Carr Hill Primary School

I Want To Paint

I want to paint a bright cherry glistening in the sunlight.
I want to paint a slippery banana waiting in the fruit bowl.
I want to paint some silky skin stroking my hand.
I want to paint some wavy leaves falling from a tree waving
in the wind.
I want to paint a jiggly satsuma rolling on the floor.
I want to paint some flamingo feathers falling from the sky.
I want to paint a shiny sky reflecting the sunlight.

Nathaniel Brewer (7)
Carr Hill Primary School

I Want To Paint . . .

I want to paint some gloopy lipstick sticky and soft.
I want to paint a gassy sun burning on a hot summer's day.
I want to paint some soft skin all over a baby's body.
I want to paint some jumpy grasshoppers jumping through the day.
I want to paint a stripy tiger waiting for its prey.
I want to paint a spooky cave filled with cobwebs and spiders.
I want to paint some crashing waves roaring like a giant whipping
                                                        things out.

Sam Wickens (7)
Carr Hill Primary School

I Want To Paint

I want to paint some shiny strawberries bathing in the relaxing sun.
I want to paint a beautiful cat sunbathing in the air.
I want to paint a fat pig playing in a splodge of mud in the sun.
I want to paint a tasty pear all juicy and delicious.
I want to paint a fast tiger, fierce and powerful and waiting
for his prey.

I want to paint a plum, yummy.
I want to paint a cotton sky full of clouds.

Melissa Sargeant (8)
Carr Hill Primary School

I Want To Paint

I want to paint some silent roses beside a sunny bank.
I want to paint a bright buttercup glowing bright when I put it
near my chin.
I want to paint some light baby skin, as pale as can be.
I want to paint some bright grass shimmering by a lake.
I want to paint a glittery goldfish swimming as proud as can be.
I want to paint a shimmery wet roof glimmering as the start
of a new day begins.
I want to paint a soothing swaying sea whooshing on the bay.

Jordanne Tomlinson (8)
Carr Hill Primary School

The Blitz

W hy was there a war in the middle of the night?
O ur world is tearing apart,
R *ing* fire brigades coming this way,
L ives are tearing apart,
D ust and dirt coming in my mouth,

W ooden beds not very nice,
A ngry people in the streets,
R unning to save their lives.

T errified and scary,
W orried and upsetting,
O ur war will never end.

Chlóe Amber Farrell (8)
Carr Hill Primary School

The Blitz

W alls were shaking
O h no not again
R evenge, I want revenge
L ives cut short
D evastated streets

W ar is horrible
A cid is all over
R un to shelter.

Liam Brady (8)
Carr Hill Primary School

The Blitz

W hat was that sound at night?
O h gosh it was a bomb,
R attling of tanks,
L oud as thunder,
D own go the buildings,

W hat a horrible night,
A smell of burning rubble all around,
R umbling thunder in the air,

T he everlasting sound of fire,
W hy did they bomb us?
O h why?

Emma Sherburn (8)
Carr Hill Primary School

The Blitz

In the middle of the night I heard the siren.
I ran down into the air raid shelter.
I was crying and shaking with fear.
I could smell gas and smoke.
I did not like the smell of the smoke.
I was just sitting there and the siren went off, I felt sick.
I felt so angry at the Germans I wanted to bomb them.
I touched the itchy blankets and itchy wooden beds.

Lewis Vardy (8)
Carr Hill Primary School

7/7 Bombings

Awful things happened on 7/7,
Fifty-two dead in the morning rush.
Was it a spin-off of 9/11?
We weren't prepared, we let people down.

Four men from the north, death their intention,
Four bombs in four rucksacks,
Four devastating, awful inventions,
We weren't prepared, we couldn't catch them.

Four men from the north went their separate ways,
Three on the tube lines, one on a bus,
They had waited now for several days,
We weren't prepared, we couldn't change their aim.

Four men from the north got out their cellphones,
Within seconds they'd detonated their bombs,
Screams of horrible terror, blood and bones.
We weren't prepared, we were giving away lives.

Four men from the north lay dead on the floors,
London's emergency services scrambled,
The drivers of victims, they opened their doors,
We weren't prepared, we were letting them die.

Finally reached by people who meant good,
The victims were taken to help and order,
Taken to a hospital like they should,
We weren't prepared, at least now we were doing right.

Awful things happened on 7/7,
Fifty-two dead in the morning rush.
Was it a spin-off of 9/11?
We weren't prepared, we let people down.

Sam Sherburn (11)
Carr Hill Primary School

The Star

I am as bright as anything
Brighter than the sun,
People watch me all night long
I travel miles and miles through space
I sometimes get tired and have a rest.

I am brighter than anything
Brighter than gold,
People love me,
They make me smile
I only show up at night,
It's my favourite time of the day
I don't like light, they can barely see me.

I am brighter than anything
Brighter than silver
The darkness is going
I better go away.

Jordan Riley (10)
Carr Hill Primary School

Snow

I gracefully fall from the frosty sky,
While I fall I twist and dance and look at the view,
I swirl in the icy wind side to side.
When I reach the silver and white ground,
I lay down on the clear blanket.

Then the happy children will come out to play,
And build me up into a big snowman,
They give me a shiny black hat,
A woollen rainbow scarf,
Two brown twigs as my arms,
My nose will be an orange carrot.

Then I will melt in the blazing sun.

Heather Bonnyman (10)
Carr Hill Primary School

I Am The Wind

When you open up an old door,
I can sneak right through.
If you don't I can go through the small keyhole,
I can play a game of hide-and-seek.
But you can't find me,
But if I don't come out to play,
I'll play with you another shivering cold day.
I live with a scorching friend,
We take a day in turns,
So we can both play with you some day some how.

I am the wind.

Victoria Stevenson (10)
Carr Hill Primary School

Music

Music is like a feather - soft and gentle,
Music is like lightning - powerful and strong,
Music is like space - fascinating, breath-taking,
Music is anything you want it to be.

Music is like a snail - slow and peaceful,
Music is like a hare - fast and upbeat,
Music is like a bird singing - jolly and happy,
Music is anything you want it to be.

Lizzi Horner (10)
Carr Hill Primary School

The Sea Turtle

I love to swim and prance around,
It's always clear blue,
The peace and quiet not a sound,
Old I am, but still fit.

The mating season has appeared,
I risk my life searching the deep blue,
I'm as small as a jellyfish, but as brave as a killer whale,
But my heart longs for a soulmate.

The deep blue is a dangerous place and full of meals.
But sharks are always near,
Their favourite meal is a seal,
Old I am, but still fit.

Nathan Gray (11)
Carr Hill Primary School

Cobwebs

I am a labyrinth but I have no centre,
I look very artistic but I have no paint
Delicate as a petal I am
Yet I can hold the weight of others.
I dance at the slightest shudder
I am still and cannot move
You can break me with a tap
And watch me be re-built
I never look the same twice
And I don't change the way I work
I wait and watch every day
I am merely a spider's web.

Sophie Riley (10)
Carr Hill Primary School

Feelings

I will hold the grainy sand as it slips through my hands.
I will hold a long, pink, satin dress which will slide off my arms.
I will hold a cute soft kitten with a nose as red as a cherry.
I will smell the freshly cut grass.
I will smell the scent of lilies in the light.
I will smell eggs and bacon in the morning.
I will hear the sea lashing against the rocks.
I will hear a newborn baby cry with fear.
I will hear soft calm music.
I will see children laughing and playing with each other.
I will see a butterfly fluttering in a field.
I will taste the melting caramel in my mouth.
I will taste a juicy hot dog on a summer's day.
I will taste a Christmas dinner on a Christmas Day.

Kennedy Brunt (10)
Carr Hill Primary School

The Fair - Cinquains

The fair
It's in Retford
It's good fun don't miss it
It is coming here for three days
Please come!

Sometimes
There's hook-a-duck
You could go on dodgems
Or there is always the fun house
Come on!

And there's
Penny machines
And cups and saucers too
There's a big inflatable slide
Let's go!

Nathan Roberts (10)
Carr Hill Primary School

The Ocean

I am the ocean the biggest and the best,
No one can beat me,
I spring in and out twice a day,
No one can catch me.

A lot of people know when I'm angry,
Stupid, silly, sly children treat me as a baby,
Other people throw rubbish and garbage at me,
I am lonely.

If I am nasty, no one plays with me,
It's as if I don't exist,
But I can be as rough as sandpaper,
Maybe no one likes me.

Luke Collingburn (10)
Carr Hill Primary School

The Sea

I run in and out all day crashing and clanging against rocks,
I can be as rough as a fierce wind, but I can be calm, very calm,
I am blue and yet clear,
When I get angry I pull people under and take their lives away.

When I am angry I smash stones to tiny bits.
I have loads of creatures who live with me.
Big, small, nasty and nice.
I am most of the time nice,
But when I get angry
I will smack people to the ground with my anger.

I have waves that will kill.
I also have waves that are nice and calm.
When I am angry I will pounce and knock you down,
I am mean and nasty
But I can be nice.

I am as cold as a bunch of ice cubes crushed up together.
I don't mean to be nasty,
I can't keep my anger in.
I have to let all the harm and pain out of me.

Guess who I am? I'm the clear blue sea.

Jasmine Smithson (10)
Carr Hill Primary School

The Zoo

Down in the zoo
There are loads of animals
There are fierce, scary lions
There are massive grizzly bears
Humungous crocodiles

A stripy tiger
Monkeys swaying from the trees
A lizard on a branch
A spider spinning a web

A slithery snake
A fluttery butterfly
A prickly hedgehog
A black and white zebra
But the biggest monkey is *you!*

Abbie Ogley (10)
Carr Hill Primary School

Lightning

I dance through the skies,
Trying to beat the rain to the ground,
I'm fierce, I'm frightening
I'm the one to be scared of.

I'm bold, I'm dramatic,
The angrier I get,
The more I destroy,
So beware of me!

I have no friends
I'm as fast as a blink,
I'm as yellow as the sun,
And I'm as frightening as a werewolf.

Amy Wonham (10)
Carr Hill Primary School

Nightmare School

I'm as black-hearted as a thief.
I'm as cruel as a powerful bully.
I'm as scary as a golden lion in your face
I am the cold-hearted nightmare school.

I'm as lethal as World War II, thirty calibre.
I'm a force not to be messed with.
I'm as dominate as an elephant,
I am the cold-hearted nightmare school.

I torture the well-behaved children every day.
I terrify them out of their tiny souls.
I'm as neck-tingling as a haunted house
I am the cold-hearted nightmare school.

I serve dead frogs and toads all of the time.
I love my playground, it's a graveyard
I am the worst school ever,
I am the cold-hearted nightmare school.

Ticha Mandy (11)
Carr Hill Primary School

Seasons

Autumn

All the leaves on the ground
because autumn is here
raking up all the leaves
then jumping in them again and again

Summer

Summer has come again
the happy time of the year
all in shorts and tops
the skylight sun shimmering in the sky

Spring

Spring is here
Seeing all the buds turning into flowers
and all the leaves on the tree
soon they will be swifting away
and all the birds will fly around

Winter

People building snowmen with cold, wet and hard snow
I have eyes as I am a snowman
I am as cold as night, shimmering
Why has winter gone, and my snowman?

Rebecca Norman (10)
Carr Hill Primary School

The Shark

I'll kill
I am deadly
Although, fish are my lunch
When I'm mad I'll devour you two
As well

I'm cool
I am the king
I rule the seven seas
I am better than King Tritan!
Oh yes!

Leighton Read (10)
Carr Hill Primary School

A Rainbow

Where does a rainbow start and end?
They're lovely colours like yellow and shiny green,
The colours shine so bright just like the sun,
The orange and yellow are so bright.

I would love to sit on top of a rainbow,
They're so sweet, just as sweet as marshmallow,
I wonder if fairies live on top of the rainbow and dust
their delicate wings,
Fairies can be very cheeky and run away and pinch their pot of gold.

I've got to find a pot of gold then I've done my mission,
Then I will be shiny again and stand out to my friends,
I will save some for my friends, my very good friends,
I'm a shiny silvery rainbow that you will see again.

Emily Slann (10)
Carr Hill Primary School

Young Writers - A Pocketful Of Rhyme Nottinghamshire

Motorbikes

Motorbikes are the best,
Beat all the cars and the rest.
Bikes will beat a car.

Cars you will not win!
They'll beat you in a second.
Bikes will thrash you too.

Motorbikes will win!
Thrashing all the rest of them.
Beating all the best.

Jakob Morvinson-Capes (10)
Carr Hill Primary School

Dream Zone

I come and haunt you every night.
Sometimes I'll fill you with horrific fright,
You cannot stop me,
You cannot stop me,
I come out to play at night,
And I have to hide at daylight,
I know what you are afraid of,
I know the monster under your bed,
And the nightmare clown I know all your secrets!

Nathan Walker (9)
Carr Hill Primary School

The Wind

I can push you over like a boxer,
I can get the dry scorching hot salty sand in your eyes,
I can knock your precious gifts out of your hands,
I can get into your home when it's locked.

I can move all the smelly
Disgusting rubbish which should be in the bin,
I can blow the salty golden sand in your clean socks,
So they will be dirty after,
I can slow you down when
You're running if I'm against you,
But I can help you when
I'm with you, like a friend.

Sam Price (10)
Carr Hill Primary School

The Scorpion

Watch out for my deadly weapons and my fierce poisonous sting,
When I am angry I could kill you in a flash,
I am never calm,
You should stay away, far away,
I am all-powerful everyone will say,
Watch out for my huge pincers,
Once I have caught you I will never let go,
I am all-powerful,
Beware!

Liam Davies (10)
Carr Hill Primary School

The Colourful Writing

As dark as the night sky.
As light as the morning sky.
As shiny as the vinyl on a car.
As dull as some rusty paint.
As big as the night moon.
As small as a toy car.
As cool as a BMX on the road.
As uncool as an old bike with a rusty body.
As colourful as a beautiful rainbow.
As drab as some old paint.

Toby Bexon (10)
Carr Hill Primary School

I Want To Paint

I want to paint a rising sunset glowing in the autumn sky
I want to paint a small delicate dandelion waving in the wind
I want to paint a spotty butterfly floating to a flower
I want to paint a field of graceful grass swaying and swishing
I want to paint a sweet, sweet orange resting in a bowl
I want to paint a beautiful bunch of grapes hanging in the big shop
I want to paint a bright sky making me feel happy
I want to paint a . . . rainbow

Chloe Marshall (7)
Carr Hill Primary School

Colours

Orange is a butterfly
Flapping his wings up and down.
Pink is a fairy
With a dark pink spark.
Blue is a cup
Getting ready for a wash.
Yellow is a sun
With a bright, bright glow.
Green is a colourful leaf
Going side to side on a dark, windy night.
Purple is a dahlia
Popping up like a pom-pom.
Red is a burning hot fire
On a hot summer's day.

Courtney Green (7)
Carr Hill Primary School

I Want To Paint

I want to paint a sweet-smelling rose growing higher and higher.
I want to paint a shimmering sunset shining in the sky.
I want to paint a bright flamingo standing still on one leg.
I want to paint soft clover waving in the grass.
I want to paint a sweet-smelling orange ready to eat.
I want to paint a small flower that has just been planted.
I want to paint a lovely swishing sky sitting still.
I want to paint a . . . rainbow.

Jemima Legge (7)
Carr Hill Primary School

Colours

Yellow is the falling brick
From an Egyptian temple.
Pink is a ballet dancer's dress
Dancing around and around.
Purple pansies swaying in the wind
In my little garden.

Fraser Ferguson-Harris (7)
Carr Hill Primary School

The Wind

I am the wind,
I can get through doors without opening them,
I can tear the leaves off trees,
I can spread fires across forests,
I can destroy your houses when I am angry,
I can sink ships but I don't mean to,
I can control the sea,
I am powerful,
I am the wind.

Joshua Gokoko (10)
Carr Hill Primary School

I Am The Sea

I go running in and out,
People play in me,
They dodge me,
But when I am angry,
I rip everything in my path,
I kill people, I don't mean it,
People scoop me up in buckets,
They feed me rubbish,
They hurt me by poisoning me,
I contain delicate animals.

I am the sea!

Jade Briers (10)
Carr Hill Primary School

The Sun

I am as hot as fire burning down a house,
I can make you take your coat off,
I can burn you and make your flowers grow,
But if you touched me you would die,
I am the star providing heat in our solar system,
I am a fireball of heat in the day,
I can shine through the window and blind you,
But the worst thing is . . .
I can give you illness for days
Be warned I am strong!
Can you guess what I am?
I am the sun.

Claudia Robinson (11)
Carr Hill Primary School

9/11

Boom went a plane flying through the sky,
Everyone was shocked and everybody cried.
One plane crashed into the Twin Towers,
All time stopped and so did the hours.

News reporters rushed to the place,
Fireman and police were on the case,
To help New York and the other people,
Where the slightest move could be lethal.

Ruth Copeland (10)
Carr Hill Primary School

The Magic Box
(Based on 'Magic Box' by Kit Wright)

I will put in my box. . .
The mystical moment of meeting my best friend Emily.
The feeling of my cheeky sister Jennifer being born.
The beautiful sight of Wolacombe's golden beach and blue sea.

I will put in the box . . .
The gorgeous taste of melting, irresistible milk chocolate.
The fantabulous smell of walking into a fish and chip shop.
The wonderful sound of my favourite band, Sugababes.

I will put in my box . . .
A celeb in an old mini, and a beggar in a long white limo.
A frog in a dog bed and a dog on a lily pad
A cute tiger on the monkey bars, and a monkey in the long grass.

My box is fashioned from
Leopard skin and sparkles and fairy wings,
With feathers on the lid and glitter in the corners
Its hinges are the red hats of pixies.

I shall snowboard in my box
On the golden sands of the Caribbean
Then drink a succulent strawberry smoothie
On the golden sand the colour of the sun.

Alice Buttery (9)
Carr Hill Primary School

The Blitz

Oh no not again, the ear-aching siren.
I heard clanging outside my room.
I fled from my bed, into the cellar,
Which felt like a freezing fridge.

I smelt the damp down in the cellar,
I rushed outside to see what was happening,
I smelt the burning and the smoke,
My mum grabbed my arm and pulled me in.

I heard the bombs and people screaming,
Fire crackling went round the city,
I also heard houses collapsing.

I felt my itchy blanket and my woollen bear too
I just wanted to throw up
I could taste ashes too.

Blyth Gray (8)
Carr Hill Primary School

The Blitz

W hat was that noise in the night?
O h gosh it was a bomb
R attling of tanks,
L oud as thunder
D own go the buildings.

W hat a horrible night
A smell of burning all around,
R umbling of thunder in the air.

T he everlasting sound of fire,
W hy did they bomb us?
O h why?

Rhiannon Mallatratt (8)
Carr Hill Primary School

The Blitz

I sit up in my bed,
Hearing the sound of a screeching siren,
Dashing downstairs into my air raid shelter.
Cuddling up to a rough blanket
Trying to fall asleep,
I can't believe it, I've left my teddy,
How will I ever sleep without it?

Charlotte Allsopp (8)
Carr Hill Primary School

Untitled

W alls were shaking
O h no bombs bombing
R oof crashing down
L and is destroyed
D estruction

W indows crashing
A nderson shelter
R umble rumble

T errified
W recked house
O dours of smoke.

Emily Cooper (8)
Carr Hill Primary School

Sunset

Sun as bright as fire
Sky as red as holly berries
Clouds like pillows floating on a bed.
Mist like a blanket over the bridge.

Demi Stanley (10)
Carr Hill Primary School

Motorcross Bike

The engine revving on the start line, like a dragster.
The wheels spinning like a spinning top.
The sound of the crowd cheering
As loud as a train screaming in a tunnel.
The sound of the gears clanking like someone's choking.
The smoke as white as snow.

Josh Mansell (10)
Carr Hill Primary School

The Blitz

Bang, crash
Explosions smash
Flickering fires
Licking flames
Smoky smells all around
My mum and dad cannot be found

Toasted houses in the street
I'm walking round in bare feet
When it stops, where will I be?
Why aren't my mummy and daddy with me?

Although I'm small I have to fight
But still no shelters, not one in sight.

With my two cats forever lost
My dad would shout at me about how much they'd cost

I wonder where my parents could be but still I wonder
What is to become of me?

I know there are many golden chances of dying
But still there is no point in crying

Will I be the only brave one, not sat like a baby crying for its mum?
I wonder what has happened to my friends
I hope that victory is round the bend.

Charlotte Hart (8)
Carr Hill Primary School

The Blitz

Thunder, lightning was everywhere,
What shall I do?
Bashing, crashing noises would not stop,
Then *bash*, one dropped on my house,
So I ran downstairs to my mum.

Then *bash, crash* it hit the church,
The flames kept kissing the walls,
So I got my bucket and went to the lake,
I filled it up with water and threw it on the church.

Bye-bye houses,
Bye-bye church,
There you go up in flames,
Bye-bye!

I got on the train,
Two hours later,
There was the countryside,
I was safe.

Aimee Flear (8)
Carr Hill Primary School

The Magic Box
(Based on 'Magic Box' by Kit Wright)

I will put in the box . . .
The magical place of the Majorca resort.
The fabulous memory of watching Forest at the ace City Ground.
The sad emotion of my great goldfish dying in its blue bowl.

I will put in the box . . .
The beautiful sound of birds singing in their wooden nests.
The smell of Nanna's super excellent cooking.
The taste of dripping honey on toast.

I will put in the box . . .
A racer on an old ship and a sailor in a sports car.
A moo of a dog and a woof of a cow.
A brum of a pig and an oink of a cool car.

My box is fashioned from
Paper and chocolate with gold and pins on the lid
and memories in the corners.
Its hinges are the tusks of rough elephants.

I shall skateboard in my box, on the skate parks of New York,
then perform on the ramps, the colour of lightning.

Jack Eaton (9)
Carr Hill Primary School

Motocross

Engine revving as loud as thunder in the dark sky
Mud spraying like a dog shaking off water
Suspension springing like flips on a trampoline
Wheel spinning like a football rolling
Speed as fast as lightning flashing across the sky.

Oliver Cooper-Bannister (10)
Carr Hill Primary School

Doctor Who

The noise of a Dalek firing his gun.
The marching of Cybermen down the street.
The buzzing of the Doctor's sonic screwdriver
The explosion of gunfire coming from the streets
Smoke coming from Torchwood Tower
The repeating noise of the Cybermen screaming, *'Delete.'*
The noise of an alien life form attacking the world.
The *'sqwatching'* of the Tardis going to another planet.

Curtis Atkinson (10)
Carr Hill Primary School

Rainbow

Red like a sweet strawberry
Yellow like a long banana
Green like a fresh kiwi
Blue like a blueberry sky
Pink like a soft peach
Orange like a bright, juicy satsuma
Purple like a dark, smooth plum
Colourful like a fresh fruit rainbow.

Reanne Broomfield (10)
Carr Hill Primary School

The Magic Box
(Based on 'Magic Box' by Kit Wright)

I will put in the box . . .
The magnificent memory of me being a mascot at Mansfield Town
and my brother showing me off to the roaring crowd.
The fabulous feeling of the golden sandy beach and building
sandcastles with my sister.
The tantalising taste of a tasty cookie melting in my mouth.

I will put in the box . . .
The mystical sound of my favourite band The Kaiser Chiefs
The smell of amazing cupcakes in the oven at 2pm
The feel of moist fabrics on my neat and tidy bed.
The roar of a scary dog and the bark of a chunky lion.

I shall eat in my box at my favourite restaurant.

Sean Revill (10)
Carr Hill Primary School

The Magic Box

(Based on 'Magic Box' by Kit Wright)

I will put in my box . . .
My funny stepbrother falling off my big bed.
The funny feeling of waking up on the first day of a new school year.
The lovely taste of beautiful home-made chips.

I will put in my box . . .
The sound of beautiful birds singing in the morning,
A fabulous place when I went on holiday to sunny Spain,
The lovely smell of Morrisons making amazing bread.

I will put in my box . . .
A cat on a lead and a dog let free,
A crying baby on a surfboard and a cool surfer in a pink pram.

My box is fashioned from chocolate and milky buttons and bread,
With beautiful hearts on the lid and friendship in the corners,
Its hinges are as sharp as a red bull.

I shall swim in my box in the Retford Sports Centre,
Then get my badges like all the other good swimmers.

Amber Caudwell (9)
Carr Hill Primary School

Evacuation

I am missing my mum and dad
And I am so sad
I hope I have got my gas mask.
Or I might breathe my last.
And I want the train to go fast
I don't want my house to get blown up.
I hope my dad has good luck
Fighting in World War II.
The train has arrived, now I feel fine
And I don't want Dad to step on a mine.

Lauren Moles (8)
Carr Hill Primary School

The Blitz

The bombs were falling,
The sirens were wailing.
Flames were licking up the walls,
Fright, fright, fright.

Smoke drifted past my nose,
Just then I froze,
I saw a flash, my house exploded,
Gone, gone, gone.

All that was left was my little teddy bear,
I love you, I love you, I love you.

I heard air raids making their noises,
I was very, very scared,
Scared, scared, *scared*.

Planes were flying above my house,
And then there was silence,
Silence, silence, silence.

Jordan Cowen (8)
Carr Hill Primary School

The Blitz

At dawn I suddenly woke,
From the window I smelt smoke.
'Come downstairs,' said my mother,
Into the cellar we hid.
The smell of smoke made me freeze from my head to my knees.

My mum said, 'Don't get scared we will be safe.'
For I could still hear the sirens going off.
The sirens got closer and closer.
The sound of that gave me the fear that my house was on fire.

Then later it was silent, we waited for a bit,
Then my mum got out from under the stairs,
The Blitz had ended!

Isobel Davis (9)
Carr Hill Primary School

The Blitz

One night in the sky,
There were lots of sparks flying.
What did I do?
Did I deserve this?
The hungry, hungry flames waiting
For me to fall.
Someone said, 'Help, help! Fire, fire!'
Where was it coming from?
How should I know?
Was it a kid?
Was it a warden?
I thought, *how should I know?*

George Loaring (8)
Carr Hill Primary School

Poppies

Poppies are shining red with a nice scent.
Poppies grow in a bright green field.
Everywhere I go I see, all the time, lots and lots of
shiny red poppies.
Poppies make some people sad as they remember
their loved ones.
Poppies, poppies make us all sad when we remember
the soldiers who died for us to live.

Chayse Hayes (8)
Carr Hill Primary School

The Magic Box

(Based on 'Magic Box' by Kit Wright)

I will put in the box . . .
My worst memory of the last time my grandad kicked the ball
before he died.
The fabulous feeling of when I scored from the halfway line
when I was just nine years old,
Granny's brilliant large white house with a dark orange door.

I will put in the box . . .
The amazing sound of Rick Astley singing 'Never Gonna Give You Up',
The delicate smell of delicious chocolate cake,
The scrumptious taste of pieces of succulent pork.

I will put in the box . . .
A super surfer in a pram and a baby on a surfboard,
A fat pig's moo and a dark brown cow's oink,
An enormous train in the sea and a fabulous ferry on a track.

My box is fashioned from bronze and metal and aluminium,
with sparkles on the lid and darkness in the corners.
Its hinges are the nails of hippos.

I shall snowboard in my box in the stormy Atlantic Ocean,
then jump on the back of a killer whale, and happily wash ashore.

Liam King (9)
Carr Hill Primary School

The Blitz

Rubble was everywhere,
Smoke made my nose tickle,
As I looked around,
My spine began to prickle.

Soon I began to cry,
As I looked at my home,
Then I looked so shy,
As I watched my house roast.

Soon I felt so bad,
As the Blitz bombed the streets,
I was looking around to find my dad,
All I saw was fire that reminded me of war.

Bethany Durham (8)
Carr Hill Primary School

The Magic Box

(Based on 'Magic Box' by Kit Wright)

I will put in my box . . .
The brilliant memory of the first time I played football,
The fabulous feeling of touching my soft jumper,
A magical place where I went on holiday in Crete.

I will put in my box . . .
The beautiful sound of my brother's guitar when my dad plays it,
A lovely smell of my wet clothes when they come out the washer,
The mouth-watering taste of home-made cakes.

I will put in my box . . .
A stripy cat on a leash and a dog running freely,
A footballer surfing and a cool surfer playing football,
A dog barking 'miaow' and a cat barking 'woof'.

My box is fashioned from cakes and cookies and chips,
With glitter on the lid and friendship in the corners
Its hinges are the horns of a fire-breathing dragon.

I shall play football in my box, in a safe street in Retford,
Then practice some cool tricks like Mr Hessey.

Rebecca Glasier (10)
Carr Hill Primary School

The Magic Box

(Based on 'Magic Box' by Kit Wright)

I will put in my box . . .
A tear of trauma trickling down my cheek,
Words of wisdom echoing through the ages,
The nest of a bird lying on the edge of a cliff.

I will put in the box . . .
A ghostly sound in a forgotten mansion,
An unbreakable claw of pure adamantium
The first snowflakes of a freezing December.

I will put in the box . . .
The sound of your pencil gliding slowly,
The first secret to be kept in silence,
Big Ben striking his first twelve.

I will put in the box . . .
Seven simple seasons including summer and spring,
A child flying a plane,
A pilot playing with toys.

My box is fashioned from
Sparkling silver, glorious gold,
Irresistible ice, furious fire,
And over one thousand years old.

I shall fly in my box
Over the Great Wall of China,
To the most outer space,
To live my life in freedom.

Jordan Wright (9)
Carr Hill Primary School

The Blitz

Stood in the middle of the street,
Watching houses collapse into piles of rubble,
Teddy bears and people's lives disintegrating.

People panicked as children died,
The smoke was rough and the fires deadly,
Houses burned, as sirens rang,
As Hitler bombed different cities and towns.

We went to shelter underground,
Planes were above the bombs fell,
Smoke in the air and little black dots,
Bigger and bigger down to the ground,
Everything demolished.

Samuel Bacon (8)
Carr Hill Primary School

When I Got Evacuated

Evacuation, evacuation, I didn't really like it.

Smoke swirled on the platform,
As the engine was eager to go.
I gazed into my mum's eyes,
I felt terrible to be leaving her,
But it had to be done.

When I jumped onto the train,
I felt nervous and scared.
There were loads of empty seats,
I picked one particular one.
In view of my mum,
As I started to cry the train set off.
I thought to myself, *where am I going?*
Will I ever see my mum again?

One girl came over to me, she sat down and said hello.
I could only see trees and trees again.
I was in a sad mood,
But I was polite and answered the girl.
She looked so much like my mum when she was young.

The train stopped so we could get some air,
As I got back on the train,
I knew I could not go back.
I sat down and wept.

Evacuation, evacuation, I didn't really like it.

Elizabeth Fidler (8)
Carr Hill Primary School

The Twin Towers

Down came the plane,
Towards the two towers,
Everybody saw it,
Panic by the pilot.

Everybody thinking
What will it do?
The plane's getting nearer,
Panic by the passengers.

Everybody worried,
Thinking, *it will hit*,
The plane getting closer,
Panic by the workers.

Everybody petrified,
As the plane hits,
Everybody running,
Panic by the citizens.

The towers are falling,
The towers are destroyed,
The towers were so beautiful,
But now they're gone.

Panic was all around,
Shouting was everywhere,
Everybody was screaming,
But now it's settled down.

Adam Flear (10)
Carr Hill Primary School

The Future

Rusty robots going back in time
Flying cabbies never earn a dime
Floating schools falling to the ground
Sidekick cats never fight their round.

Uranus keeps crashing into the sun
Baby robots having such robotic fun
Magic spells always start big fires
People always burn old useless tyres.

Aaron Bradley (10)
Carr Hill Primary School

It Was On TV

It was on TV, everyone knew,
Everyone saw it
It wasn't Roo.

C Ronaldo wanted the foul
Rooney gave him an evil scowl
Rooney pushed him as hard as he could
He hit the deck with a great big thud.

The one diving on the floor
The one they call Carvalho
He got up without a wince
Rooney's hated him ever since.

James Hudson (10)
Carr Hill Primary School

Caterpillar Poem

I saw a little caterpillar
I went to say hello
As he slid across the leaf
His body was all yellow.

As he looked up at me from the leaf
He gave a little grin,
I said, 'How are you doing?'
And he said, 'How have you been?'

Laura Murray (10)
Carr Hill Primary School

Spiderweb Poem

I saw a spiderweb
I couldn't see the spider
I thought it was dead.

The silk was really strong
There were flies caught up
They couldn't break free,
Then I saw a spider,
It looked meanly at me.

Then lots of spiders struck down on me,
They caught me and captured me
But best of all I broke free.

On the way home I saw the colour chrome in the air
Guess what it was, a spiderweb,
This time I couldn't break free,
So that was the end of me.

Leon Savastio-Birkbeck (10)
Carr Hill Primary School

Autumn Time

Leaves are blowing beneath my feet,
A magpie sat down on the bench seat,
I'm out here freezing cold,
As the wind blew, I saw many leaves that unrolled.

Red, yellow and brown leaves are all scattered around,
All is silent, except a windy whistling sound,
My nice and warm house is right ahead,
I can't wait to snuggle up tight in my comfortable bed.

Olivia Zeraati (10)
Carr Hill Primary School

Rainbow

A rainbow comes when it rains
It doesn't take any pains
Oh what a sight
When it takes flight
And colours are all it contains

A rainbow is always up high
Always up high in the sky
It never comes down
Down to the ground
When the rain stops it's goodbye.

Tamara Cartwright (10)
Carr Hill Primary School

All Alone

I walked around the lifeless street
With crispy leaves blowing at my feet
It was empty with not one sound
Nothing in the air and nothing on the ground

I felt so lonely with not a soul in sight
All that lay ahead was a flickering light
I felt a shiver down my spine
The light got brighter with a blinding shine

I shouted for help but there was no reply
I felt unsure and started to cry
I felt like shrivelling into a ball
As no one could hear my helpless call.

I heard a familiar but frightened voice
Should I run? I had no choice
I ran and ran as far as I could
But in front of me my best friend stood.

A warm feeling rushed to my brain
I'll never get lost or lose you again.

Ellie Hatt (10)
Carr Hill Primary School

Spiderweb

I saw a spiderweb
I couldn't see the spider
I thought the spider was dead

The thread was really strong
There were loads of flies caught up.

Then the spider came from nowhere.
It wrapped up all the flies.
Then went back into camouflage.

Matt Tunnard (10)
Carr Hill Primary School

Change - Cinquains

Blue, red
Black spots and hair
Eating all the big leaves
Changing, changing, changing their lives
It's gone

It's gone
Caterpillar
Oh it has gone, where to?
Will it come back or will it change?
How? How?

What now?
How have you changed?
Oh where did you go to?
To rest in my cocoon and change
But how?

Tell me
If you do know
Will you come back again
As a beautiful butterfly?
Bye-bye.

Lauren Hotson (11)
Carr Hill Primary School

Caterpillar

Beautiful as can be,
All the colours you can see
Hangs off a delicate tree
What creature is it you tell me.

Can you see
How beautiful they can be
They land so softly on a tree
They look so nice to me

Their colours can be blue
They can be nice to you
The circle will create something new
They will wait around but will not queue.

They might be by
They are a bit shy
Crawls up a tree so high
They turn into a butterfly.

Lauren Tong (10)
Carr Hill Primary School

The Twin Towers

An ordinary day took place,
The two Twin Towers started to break,

I ran down from the top of the stairs,
My work friends were following me in pairs,
We rushed to the bottom, we could not see,
All the smoke was blinding me!

Fortunately I survived,
But my work friends have sadly died.

Katie O'Sullivan (10)
Carr Hill Primary School

The Magic Box

(Based on 'Magic Box' by Kit Wright)

I will put in my box . . .
An army, chocolate land and lots of guns, lots of toys,
cool music and cool cars.

I will put in my box . . .
A surfboarder on a skateboard and a skateboarder on a surfboard.
A baby on a motorbike and a motorbiker in a pram.

My box is fashioned from ice, metal, chocolate, guns,
PS2 games and electric barbed wire.

I shall play army in my box.
In the darkest, thickest and lushest jungle playing army
and after that we will do paintballing in a deep green forest.

Joseph Murphy (10)
Carr Hill Primary School

The Magic Box

(Based on 'Magic Box' by Kit Wright)

I will put in the box . . .
The grip of a gun on the dead battlefield,
Fire from a gattling gun pinning its enemies,
The weight of a helmet pushing your head.

I will put in the box . . .
A bullet travelling at the speed of lightning,
Track of a tank filling the roads with dust,
Poseidon's golden trident.

I will put in the box . . .
The deathness of a tank rocket exploding its only opponent.
The boom of the Earth obliterating,
The bright beaming light of a flare.

I will put in the box . . .
An army man with a guitar,
A pop star with a gun,
The red eclipse of a summer night.

My box is fashioned from
Water, fire, ice and air
With burning flames on the lid
And icicles on the corners.

I will fight in my box
The giants that roam the land fearless,
The evil communist army,
The smashing Saxons.

Iago Thomas (9)
Carr Hill Primary School

Senses

I saw the sun
At the break of dawn
I saw a bird
Greeting the morn

I saw a bowl of cornflakes
When it was breakfast time
I saw a zingy lemon
Wedged between a lime

I saw my school folder
Sitting in the hall
I saw the tree outside my window
Standing proud and tall

I saw the pasta
In a dish
I saw a star
Make a wish

I appreciate
The things I see
For I cannot hear things
I am deaf you see.

Katy Adams (9)
Carr Hill Primary School

The Beach

The crashing of the waves
As I surf on the sea
The beach is deserted
No one can see me

I'll do the dance of the dolphins
As they swim through the blue
The song of the gulls
As they come into view

Back on the beach
As the tide rolls away
I stand there silently
At the end of the day

Jamie Jenkins (9)
Carr Hill Primary School

The Magic Box

(Based on 'Magic Box' by Kit Wright)

I will put in my box . . .
A tickle from the green grass sweeping below my feet,
Whispers of the wind passing through the trees.

I will put in my box . . .
The last breath of an old grandad,
A sad memory from an old film,
Soft sand escaping through my fingertips,
One drop of ice-blue water trickling down my hand.

I will put in my box . . .
The great shout of anger wounding my soul,
The first notes of a lullaby melting the heart.
A jar of silence spreading throughout the sky,
An echo bouncing against the watery walls of a cave.

I will put in my box . . .
A grumble of a gurgling belly ready for its lunch,
The twinkling eye of a baby ready to cause mischief,
A swish of a pony's golden locks passing through the wind,
A thirteenth month and an eighth day.

My box is fashioned from
Glass, silver and ice,
With diamonds on the lid and wishes in the drawers.
Its handle is the sceptre of a wizard,
Its catch is the hook of a pirate.

I shall meet mystical creatures in my box
I'll dance the great ocean with the pixies and elves,
I will sing the sky song with the fairies and banshees,
Also I will fly the world with the glorious unicorns
And sleep silently with the snoring gnome.

Becki Partridge (9)
Carr Hill Primary School

The Sound Collector

(Based on 'The Sound Collector' by Roger McGough

'A stranger called at midnight
Dressed in all black and grey
Put every sound into a box
And carried them away'

The scribble of a pencil
The miaow of a cat
The tick of a clock
The whack of a bat

The cackle of a witch
The bubbling of cakes
The steam of an iron
The squealing noise it makes

The flap of a book
The snap of a stick
The football right in front of you
The swoop of a kick

The pitter-patter of raindrops
Taking over the sky
When the wind hits the washing
It swooshes when it flies.

'A stranger called at midnight
He didn't give his name
He left us only silence
Life will never be the same'.

Jasmine Cross (9)
Carr Hill Primary School

The Sound Collector

(Based on 'The Sound Collector' by Roger McGough)

A stranger came this morning
All dressed in grey and white,
He put our sounds into a box
And it took him till late night.

The screeching from the baby,
The howling of the dog,
The crashing of the cutlery,
The child jumping on the log.

The whistling of the kettle,
The banging of the drawer,
And the noise that you then really like,
That then never returns anymore.

The fuzzing from the television,
The fighting with the cats,
The muddy, muddy boots,
Which have been scraped on mats.

The snoring of the sleeping children,
In their soft beds,
The tweeting of kitchen birds,
Feeling their soft cuddly heads.

The crackling of tin foil,
The munching from the dad,
The moaning of the mother,
The parrots squawking mad.

A stranger came this morning,
He took all our sounds away,
He left us all so peaceful,
It will be strange every day.

Emily Rewston (9)
Carr Hill Primary School

The Sound Collector

(Based on 'The Sound Collector' by Roger McGough)

'A stranger called this morning
Dressed all in black and grey
Put every sound into a bag
And carried them away'

The ping of a microwave
The flicker of a fire
The beep of an oven
The zap of TV wire

The chopping of a knife
The sshh of a running tap
When the kitten comes home
The cat flap goes flap, flap

The hiss of a frying pan
The creak of the stairs
When Mum goes shopping
She buys juicy pears

'A stranger called this morning
He didn't leave his name
He left us only silence
Life will never be the same'.

Jessica Speirs (10)
Carr Hill Primary School

The Sound Collector

(Based on 'The Sound Collector' by Roger McGough)

'A stranger called this morning
Dressed all in black and grey
Put every sound into a bag
And carried them away'

The rumble of a lawnmower
The creak of the door
The tinkle on the bathroom tap
The shuffle on the floor

The bark of a dog
The clink of a gate
The crash of a window
Oh no it's going to break

The vibration of the PC
The crunch of the leaves
The shake of the pepper
I think I'm going to sneeze.

The zoom of a car flying past
Indicating to the right
The crash of a lorry into a wall
What an amazing sight

The flicking of a boring book
The splash of a speedboat on the sea
The crackle of Velcro
The crack of a broken knee.

'A stranger called this morning
He didn't leave his name
He left us only silence
Life will never be the same'.

Mitchell Gleaden (9)
Carr Hill Primary School

The Sound Collector

(Based on 'The Sound Collector' by Roger McGough)

'A stranger called this morning
Dressed all in black and grey
Put every sound into a bag
And carried them away'

The sound of a bell,
The creak of a door,
The bark of a dog,
The sound of a knock.

The scribble of a pencil,
The scratching of a cat,
When you walk in the snow,
The crunching noise it makes.

The sizzling of sausages,
The dong of the clock,
The bubble going pop,
And the tick of a clock.

The pitter-patter of the rain,
On the window edge,
When you let the water go,
The sound of the drain.

'A stranger called this morning
He didn't leave his name
He left us only silence
Life will never be the same'.

Danielle Hammond (10)
Carr Hill Primary School

Sunset

Built in the evening,
Goes into the white soft clouds
I'm scared if it drops
Get to places and quicker
Nervous because how high it is.

Daniel Moody (10)
Carr Hill Primary School

The Magic Box

(Based on 'Magic Box by Kit Wright)

I will put in the box . . .
The magnificent memory of getting my tropical fish.
The funny feeling of going to a cool school.
The opposite place of the Odeon.

I will put in my box . . .
The zooming sound of speedy cars.
The terrific smell of cooling cookies.
The lovely lasagne taste.

I will put in my box . . .
The woof of a cat and the miaow of a dog.
The moo of a pig and the oink of a cow.
The quack of a sheep and the baa of a duck.

My box is fashioned from
Soothing silk and chocolate and macaroni,
with spikes on the lid and sequins in the corners.
Its hinges are the pointy tusk of an elephant.

I shall ice skate on the slippery ice of Antartica,
then perform some tricks as good as in 'Strictly Come Dancing'.

Kristien Gregory (9)
Carr Hill Primary School

The Magic Box

(Based on 'Magic Box' by Kit Wright)

I will put in the box . . .
The magical match of me scoring a hat-trick against Forest B,
The rattling rumbling at attractive Alton Towers.
The delicious soothing taste of smoked salmon,
The exciting emotions I would get playing for Liverpool,
The magical memory of signing for brilliant Babworth Rovers.
A noisy duck playing tennis and brilliant Roger Federer swimming.

My box is fashioned from gold,
Chocolate and pizza, with footballs on the lid
And wishes in the corners.
Its hinges are the hairy skin of a dog.

I shall play cricket at Edgbaston Cricket Ground
And hit the ball as hard as Steven Gerrard shoots it.

James Bacon (9)
Carr Hill Primary School

The Train

In the afternoon noisily a train came.
Loud train stopped and pulled its horn.
Desperate people ran on train.
Crushed, horn was pulled, off to London.
Stopped quickly desperate people get off now.

Ryan Spires (10)
Carr Hill Primary School

Graffiti

Early in morning
Graffiti ruins nice walls
Spiders on nice walls
I see people scrubbing walls
I don't like graffiti.

Jakob Higson (10)
Carr Hill Primary School

Storm

Late in afternoon
Buildings were ripped down all day
People were ready
It was like a bad rhino
It all got destroyed in days.

Richard Caldwell (10)
Carr Hill Primary School

Nightfall

Night falls, it's late
I should be in bed.
But I stand here at my window
To watch the world go by instead . . .

Stars sparkle, the moon shines
Lighting up the sky.
I hear the sound of footsteps
And the voices of passers-by.

Dogs bark, cats call
What a dreadful din!
Does no one at all hear them
Asking to come in?

Eyes close, head droops
I can no longer stay.
Turn off the light, get into bed
To dream the night away.

Rhiannon Smith (11)
Carr Hill Primary School

The Fireworks

Twinkle fireworks being let off
Sparkling through in the wonderful and beautiful starry sky.
Red, orange, yellow and pink colours of the fireworks.
Catherine wheels swirling through the air
And sparklers twinkling everywhere.
Wherever you go you will see light.
Fireworks being let off one at a time.
Then we see them blast out loud.
Wonderful, wonderful fireworks
Crash, bang, crackle
Here they go.

Nicole Patara (8)
Middleton Primary School

Help

H ow many children have to die each day?
E very supply is needed
L ove is what they need
P lease help us.

Amin Ahmadi (8)
Middleton Primary School

Countryside

Green grass, fresh air
You will find rabbits there
Screaming, shouting, running around
That's where you will find a greyhound
Birds and foxes in the wood
Running away from Robin Hood
Cows grazing in the meadow
A female deer is called a doe
If you like to go outside
You will go wild in the countryside.

Isabel Prince (8)
Middleton Primary School

Oak Trees

O ak trees grow very old,
A nd they have lots of leaves.
K ick it and you'll break your leg.

T he oak trees are very big,
R are trees can be oak trees.
E ggs are softer than them,
E vil people try to kill them.
S ome people are very nice.

A pples don't grow on them,
R abbits like to eat the acorns,
E ating acorns munching loudly.

B ugs live in the bark,
I n the autumn leaves fall off.
G ood people look after them.

John Mikhail (8)
Middleton Primary School

Fireworks

Rockets shoot up to the stars and spacemen.
Rockets whizz and they're very fast.
Rockets sparkle.
Catherine wheels spin and they're very pretty.
Catherine wheels are colourful.
Screamers scream with the children.
Screamers are very noisy.
Sparklers sparkle and twinkle,
Fireworks are pretty.

Georgia Sheridan-Parker (7)
Middleton Primary School

Trees

Blossom grows in the spring
On the trees.
Blossom looks good on everything.
Leaves are green and turn brown in the winter.
In the winter the leaves fall off onto the ground.
When it is winter all the trees are blowing.
In the winter it is very cold.
In the summer the leaves grow back and turn green again.

Aston Morgan (8)
Middleton Primary School

Fireworks

Rockets booming in the air,
Sparklers sparkling at night,
Bonfires burning everywhere.

Screamers screaming everywhere,
Everyone is screaming at the Catherine wheel,
All the fireworks are colourful,
The wind is freezing like ice,
The sky is colourful,
Screamers let up in the air,
Bonfire Night is fun and cold.

Inshaal Akbar (8)
Middleton Primary School

The Horse

On a cold winter's day
I once saw a beautiful horse
He was black and white
He was galloping really fast
He was wild, his mane was falling back as he ran
He was breathing fast, steamy breath.
He was swishing his long tail
He stopped and came over to me
I stroked him
I got on him and rode him
He went faster than a speedboat
He took me to my farm
I kept him.

Aimee Clay (7)
Middleton Primary School

Doctor Who Poem

Would you like to come with me?
To travel in the Tardis,
I'll name some monsters.
Here I go . . .
Autons, Casandra and the gelth too,
Slitheens are coming after you.
A Cyberman's catchphrase is 'delete',
Plus they are tricky to defeat.
But when it comes to facing a Dalek
It will turn you into over-cooked garlic.
Lucky the Doctor's still around,
To give the Daleks a whooping pound.
Plus destroy the Cybermen,
I bet they won't be back again.
Destroying both is very tricky
Also it is very sticky,
But he'd better make it snippy.
Anyway as I was saying
Back to monster mayhem.
Jagrefess/reapers/empty child too
Margret, Slitheen is back in town
Trinny and Susannah are going down.
Dalek Emperor is on the move,
Sycorax spaceship is coming too
I think I saw a sister cat
Now Casandra's coming back.
First an alien now a wolf,
Oh! they've all got me now
No!

Joshua Stables (8)
Middleton Primary School

The RSPCA

The RSPCA shelters are extremely noisy and busy.
Dogs make most of the noise by barking at other animals.
Cats that like to purr all over you every day.
Horses that make a noise by galloping and neighing.
Geese that run after people and peck at them when people
come too close.
Guinea pigs that squeak and sometimes bite, it really hurts.
Rabbits that kick when you pick them up it hurts too.
There are lots of deer whose spots are white.
There are lots of animals.
The saddest thing is when the animal has to be put down.
The RSPCA are the kindest people.
They love animals and so do I.

Amelia Lewin (7)
Middleton Primary School

Bonfire Night

Children screaming when they hear the loud sounds.
Sparklers sparkling in the moonlight.
Colourful rockets exploding in the dark sky.
Bonfire shooting towards the twinkling white stars.
Catherine wheels going round in circles.
Red, orange, yellow and pink are the colours of the fireworks.

Junaid Aslam (8)
Middleton Primary School

Fireworks

Sparklers sparkling like stars.
Rockets shooting into space
Catherine wheels spinning, spinning.
Screamers screaming in the air.
Fireworks shooting into space and making lovely colours.
Rockets exploding in the air
Catherine wheels spinning as fast as lightning.
Sparklers sparkling like bright stars.
Screamers screaming, very, very loudly.

Gemma Pearson (7)
Middleton Primary School

Autumn Leaves

Autumn leaves are falling
Falling from the sky.
Blowing in the breeze
In the sky so high.
Red, green and yellow and brown.
A spiky shape
The tree goes to sleep
All winter long.
They sleep and sleep and sleep,
All day and all night
They wake up in the spring.

Robyn Atkinson (7)
Middleton Primary School

Pirates

Pirates always want to kill other pirates to get their treasure.
All they want is treasure but they have to fight for it.
Pirates are good fighters sometimes they try to fight the captain
But the captain is too powerful.
Then they have to do what the captain says.

Damon Wright (8)
Middleton Primary School

My Family

My dad is funny
Like a bunny.

My brother is annoying
And also boring
He's always lying.

My mum is always buying
Fancy dresses and shoes.

Now we come to me
And I am a dancer
A clarinet player.

Naomi Squire (8)
Middleton Primary School

The Feast

Cheese pizza, the best I have seen,
Yummy chocolate tasting sweet
Chips in a tomato sauce,
Strawberries nice and sweet.

Nice, lovely, hot chicken curry.
Crunchy chocolate biscuits with cream.
Giant big pumpkin, juicy flavour.

Husnain Rasool (7)
Middleton Primary School

The Feast

Chewing lovely strawberries with cream.
Munching orange the biggest I've seen.
Eating sweets with sugar and salt.
Making a mess with sloppy custard that might be my fault.
Hard, bright green cucumber
Milk chocolate hard as rock in the freezer.
Vanilla sponge sitting on the plate,
Rosy apples juicy and sweet
I ate it late at night.
Hot chilli chicken curry
Lots of Italian-perfect cheesy pizzas.
Yummy chocolate chip cakes.
Gigantic vanilla-strawberry sponge
Lovely crunchy rock hard dumplings.
Sweet, ripe, juicy, tomato, chewy chicken in my tum,
Green, squishy, sloppy bean soup.

Katherine Griffin-Pearce (7)
Middleton Primary School

The Feast

Chocolate ice cream that you've never seen.
Cucumber lovely and green.

Eggs fried on a hob.
Strawberries piled up high with lots of sugar.

Beautiful steamed puddings,
Giant dumplings piled up high.
Toad-in-the-hole with lots of vegetables.

Rebecca Griffin-Pearce (7)
Middleton Primary School

Fireworks

Fireworks banging up into the cold winter's sky
Catherine wheels swirling on the fence
Screamers screaming in people's ears
Rockets bombing in the cold sky
Sparklers twinkling in people's hands

I was scared at first
But now I am fine
The fireworks are wicked
I am getting to like them now

My friend is scared
And I say
'I was scared but now I am not,'
Then my friend said
'You are right!'

We watched the fireworks together
Blue, yellow, green and red.

William Russell-Fishwick (9)
Middleton Primary School

The Beautiful Beach

My hair sways in the salty sea breeze.
The pebbles and shells scratch my knees.
The sun shines across the sea
It makes me rub my hands with glee.
Children laugh and children play,
Children have fun all day,
Crabs crawl across the sand,
People stand on rocks to view the land.

Emily Kirk (8)
Middleton Primary School

Chocolate Is Lovely

C reamy, milky
H ot chocolate, cold chocolate
O h tasty chocolate
C hocolate melting on your tongue
O h lovely chocolate
L ovely tasty types of chocolate
A hh the best chocolate
T wixs, Twirls melting on my tongue
E verybody loves chocolate.

Lauren Hammond (8)
Middleton Primary School

Fruit And Vegetables

Apples are juicier and bananas are creamier
So strawberries are sweeter and oranges smell like flowers.
Potatoes are so big, tomatoes are juicier
So carrots are hard and cabbage is soft.
Cauliflower looks like flowers.

Darnell Nugent (7)
Middleton Primary School

Being Friends

B eing friends is a wonderful thing.
E very day I feel excited because I have a friend and don't feel lonely.
I t is hard leaving a friend.
N othing matters to me, just me and my friend.
G ood it is just me and my friend together.

F riends can break up and bully sometimes, never mind
we are still friends.
R eady for a new day me and my friend will play.
I 'll never forget my friend.
E veryone bullies me but me and my friend will
N ever bully, ever.
D oing exciting things is really fun with my friend.
S o me and my friend will never break up.

Sena Mamurekli (8)
Middleton Primary School

The King's Strange Demands

The King ordered the cook to cook,
And the horrible pirate to present his hook.
Of course the pirate was not that sort of man,
But suddenly started to hum and cry, cry,
The King ordered him to give his hook
Or the cook would put him into the hot pot.
But, as he put his finger in the pot,
The pirate ran away and started to plot,
They caught him, he started to rot.
His crew let him go,
They caught them all and crashed in a wall
And there showed all the gold.

Tamara Falcone (7)
Middleton Primary School

Summer

S and
U mbrellas away
M e and my
M um
E nd of summer
R ainbows.

Morgan Wills (8)
Middleton Primary School

Rainbow

R ainbow colours brightening up the sky.
A rainbow's colours always look very high.
I n the day or in the night always looking very bright.
N ow and again the rainbow's light shines and shimmers in the night.
B lue is my favourite colour in the rainbow, who knows
O ver the rainbow nobody goes.
W hen it's raining and the sun is out there's always a rainbow about.

Abigail Ensor (7)
Middleton Primary School

Summer

S ummer is my favourite season.
U mbrellas not around
M um, Mum ice cream please.
M um, Mum holiday on the beach please.
E veryone yippee there's no school.
R un summer is over.

Alina Akhter (8)
Middleton Primary School

Fabulous Fireworks

Watching the fireworks *bang! Bang!*
Watch the screaming screamers zooming into the clouds.

Watch the rockets fly higher than mountains and higher than clouds,
Higher than anything you see.

Zoom, zoom, whee, whoosh, watch the fireworks fly.

Bang, boom, scream, screech, see the colours in the dark.

George Burton (8)
Middleton Primary School

The Chocolate Fountain

Chocolate is a tasty treat
Chocolate is my favourite
I am a chocoholic
I love chocolate more than anything.
I have a chocolate fountain!
And I can make chocolate strawberries
And chocolate marshmallows.
Chocolate melting on my tongue.

Laura Smedley (7)
Middleton Primary School

Artist

A rt flashing in my eyes.
R ainbow colours in the sky.
T he pictures looking fantastic.
I n the bright colours I feel safe and warm.
S cissors cutting through the colourful paper.
T extile weaving on the wall.

Ayesha Azad (8)
Middleton Primary School

Cricket

C ricket balls hitting wickets faster than an English motorway.
R icky Ponting smashing balls every day.
I an Bell scoring hundreds.
C ollingwood catching stormers.
K evin Peiterson smacking sixes.
E xplosive hitting by Flintoff.
T he wickets always coming from Gough.

Nicky Kirkwood (8)
Middleton Primary School

Bonfire Night

B angers go boom
O range rockets zooming in the air
N oisy fireworks go bang
F lames firing everywhere
I like the rockets the best
R oman candles spraying out flames
E at the food while you can.

Scott Skerritt (8)
Middleton Primary School

Ballet

Ballet is fun for all of us,
With tutus,
And ballet shoes,
You dance around to music.
You twirl and swirl,
And jump in the air.
Ballet is fun for all of us.
Everyone, everywhere.

Simran Trevett-Singh (7)
Middleton Primary School

Fabulous Fireworks

Fireworks shooting high into the dark blue sky.
Catherine wheels spinning round and round as fast as a cheetah.
Sparklers spitting out different glittering colours.
The fireworks burst and fall to the ground.
Fireworks screeching and screaming in the dark night sky.
Beautiful roman candles sparkling in the green grass.
Children watching in the school grounds and some watching from
their windows.

Libby Scutts (8)
Middleton Primary School

Football

F ootball makes me become aggressive and very hyper
'O n the head'
'O h goal!'
T he ball is straight in the back of the net!
B icycle kick, wow!
A round the post and off the pitch, *ooh*
L ook, extra player, not fair!
L ove footie? I do.

Ben Upjohn (8)
Middleton Primary School

On The Beach

When I went on holiday I ran to the beach
Paddling in the cold water with sand on my feet.

When I'd finished in the sea I got my bucket and spade
And I asked my dad if I could bury him with my little spade!

Molly Round (7)
Middleton Primary School

Who's Ugly?

The monster was big.
He was ugly,
He lived in the depths of the sea.
He had twenty-two legs and feet.
A mouth where his chin ought to be.
He was covered with seaweed,
He had smelly toes,
With a bump at the end of his nose.
He was really smelly,
He had three eyes,
Nobody liked him in the sea.

Rahuldeep Bawa (8)
Middleton Primary School

The Feast

I munch juicy red strawberries
Lovely blackberries

Ice cream so yummy
All goes in my tummy

I eat a lot of jelly
Rice in my belly

I crunch Turkish delight
I eat bacon at night

My starter was jam
Just then I bit ham

Blackcurrant crumble
Makes my tummy rumble

Lashings of ice cream
I think it's all just a dream.

Sumeyye Esil (8)
Middleton Primary School

The Feast

Chocolate cake is so yummy
Pizza goes down to my tummy

My favourite is jelly
Strawberries are already in my belly

I munch Turkish delight
I eat rice in the morning light

Blackcurrant crumble
Makes my tummy rumble

Lots of delicious dumplings
Enormous orange pumpkins

I had caramel custard
A tasty sandwich with mustard.

Samerah Iqbal (8)
Middleton Primary School

The Feast

Lovely fish served in a dish.
Reddish apples like a wish.
Gorgeous lamb with a lot of ham
A little bite of Turkish delight.
Lots of jelly in my belly.
Fabulous quince with hot mince.
Strawberries and cream oh give me some please.
Loads of stew I need to chew
Ice cream and sweets and hundreds more treats.

Alice Porter **(7)**
Middleton Primary School

The Sun And Sky

The sun and the sky are always together.
I really like the sun and the sky
The sun is a hot ball of fire.
The sky is like a blue sea.

Ishrat Hussain (7)
Middleton Primary School

Weather

Rain splashing on the ground,
Making puddles so much bigger.

Sun beaming on the Earth,
Making people so much hotter.

Tornado whirling round so much,
Up goes everything in its way.

Sun beaming on the Earth,
Making people so very much hotter.

Alex Chamberlain (7)
Middleton Primary School

Friends

Talisha breaks all of her toys and chases after boys.
Scott is always hot and helps a lot.
Levar has a guitar and in his car he travels far.
Lathanyel likes bacon and his toy was taken.
Ben has a hen and a nice red pen.
Zain went to Spain in an aeroplane.
I went to the shop to get some pop.
Isaac wiggles his hips and did I tell you he skips?
Aston gave me a chip, it made me sick.

Tamika Gayle (8)
Middleton Primary School

Football Crazy

Football, football, football mad
Football is crazy
Sometimes football can be sad.
I watch football every day.
Football is the best
Football is the test
I play football every day.
Because football is great.
Football is healthy for you, it keeps you fit.
I've loved football since I was one
Because football is my favourite sport.

Lucy Bradley (7)
Middleton Primary School

The Feast

Chocolate melted with cream on top of a biscuit.
Chips with tomato sauce on.
Curry on the stove choking with the scent
Crisps with vinegar on the top
Crunchy crisps on a lovely gleaming plate.
Chicken on the stove cooking like a volcano.
A lovely pizza cooking.
Oranges stacked up high like a volcano.

Hamza Tahir (8)
Middleton Primary School

The Feast

Tasty apple crumble with cream and strawberries.
Lovely, red, wobbly jelly with fantastic ice cream.
Lots of custard with cake and toffee raisins with oranges.

Phabian Graham (7)
Middleton Primary School

The Feast

At the start of the feast I'm as hungry as a beast.
Rabbit stew I might as well take a bite or two.
Tomato sauce on everything of course!
Chocolate fountain as big as a mountain.
Cakes galore and so much more!
I'm full to the brim I can fit no more in.

Mollie Newth (8)
Middleton Primary School

The Feast

Lovely apple pie in a boiling oven.
I wish there was blackberry pie with custard and cream.
I wonder if there is but I am sure gorgeous wobbly jelly
                                        sitting on a pot.
Lovely strawberries sitting on a pot.
Custard and cream waiting to be put on blueberry crumble.
Pepperoni pizza sitting on a silver plate.
Sausages sizzling in the kitchen waiting to go in my tum.

Sophia Dryden (7)
Middleton Primary School

The Feast

Strawberries and cream more than I've ever seen.
Chicken curry and rice *mmm* that sounds nice.
Red rosy apples sweetened with honey.
Milky chocolate coins as golden as money.
My tummy rumbles at the pizza delight.
There is even more, there is more tonight.
Brown, crispy, chicken drumsticks with wonderful soft insides.
Huge swans covered in gravy and mint leaves.
Crumbling biscuits with melting chocolate in my mouth.

Emma Hinnells (8)
Middleton Primary School

The Feast

Apple pie and custard in a big bowl
Brown yolky eggs piled up in piles.
Big juicy strawberries in a big bowl.
My tummy rumbles when I see juicy pineapple.
Lovely pizza cooking in the oven and it smells beautiful.
Vanilla ice cream melting in your mouth.
Sausages sizzling in the oven.
Crumbling biscuits in a huge bowl.

Callum Brown (8)
Middleton Primary School

The Feast

A lovely fish on a dish.
The taste of fish goes down
My throat like a boat.

Strawberries with clean cream
Fit for a queen.

Egg and yolk
Then a drink of Coke.

Custard and cream,
It is a dream.

Munch a pie at night.

Alice Mai Sheridan-Parker (7)
Middleton Primary School

The Feast

Munching great pizza with tomato sauce.
Do I want it? Well of course!

Nibbling only tasty chips like a mouse
Only doing it in your own house.

Eating delicious chicken curry
Swallowing it in your very own tummy.

Gobbling lots of cheesy pizza
With lots of lovely tomato sauce.

Munching great hot chicken
With lots of pepper on the top.

Biting my lovely hot burger
With some mayonnaise on it.
Eating nice lovely pumpkin.

Ibraheem Belim (8)
Middleton Primary School

The Feast

Rosy red strawberries piled upon a shiny plate.
Spiky pineapples surrounded by dates.
Chips being dipped in scarlet red ketchup.
Apple pie with a big blob of custard.
Chicken nuggets with a big bowl of barbecue sauce.
Gigantic biscuits warm on a big plate.

Olivia Rose Janmaat (7)
Middleton Primary School

The Feast

Sausages, brown and juicy stacked up on a plate
with scrumptious chips that I can dip.
Lumps of dumplings that I can munch with my lunch
and chicken nuggets that I can nibble.
Chocolate biscuits, mountains of them that I can crunch.
Pepperoni pizza that's Italian and perfect to bite all night.
My tummy's still rumbling and I see a chocolate pudding
To finish my meal I'll have a banana that I can peel.

Jack Mee (8)
Middleton Primary School

The Feast

Tearing the lovely roast chicken.
Slicing the beautiful egg.

Rip the wonderful hot bacon.
Munch the lovely cherries.

Have a gobble of melted hot chocolate cake.
Have a munch of hot apple pie with the hot custard.

Chew the dumplings in the hot soup.

Shayna McPherson (7)
Middleton Primary School

The Feast

Chocolate ice cream the best I've seen.
Strawberries with nice cream.
Rice it sounds nice.
Chicken curry cooked in a hurry.
Chips swelling my lips.

Daniel Andrew (8)
Middleton Primary School

The Feast

Munching strawberries juicier than I've ever seen.
Having chicken curry it's so hot I just feel like flying away.
Chomping biscuits on a plate but can't believe how many
                                                    crumbs it makes.
Gobbling soft dumplings in my hungry tum.
Munching hot, hot sausages it's so nice.

Thomas Judson (7)
Middleton Primary School

Untitled

The rain crawled down the window pane
As the raindrop stared at the glass,
As a bat screeched round in circles,
The wind howled through the stormy sky.

A pebble whispered through the haunted mansion
As a girl screamed herself up the stairs.

The night sniggered like a roaring lion leaping through lightning.
As a shadow winked like a ghost in the spooky sky.

Amy Ashmore (10)
St Peter's CE Primary School, East Bridgford

I Shivered

The dreaming dawn yawned and silently dreamt of nothing,
And I shivered.

The night crept up on the daylight like a cat stalking its prey,
And I shivered.

The morning leapt frantically in to midnight place
As alarm clock broke the silence,
And I shivered.

The sea rumbled, roaring ravenously
And I felt a shiver up my spine.

Luchia Ecott (10)
St Peter's CE Primary School, East Bridgford

Haunted Poem

The moss shivered silently like a
Freezing frosty snowflake on the
Cold colossal wall.

The laughing leaf swung to and fro,
Trying to escape the harsh breeze.

The wind cried in the sheer
Sharpness of the freezing frost
As the ground groaned in pain.

Flowers leapt in the wind trying
To shake off the icicles hanging
From their perfect petals.

Creepily the still stars winked in
The musty misty sky.

Heavily, the mean moon pushed
The shining sun as the clouds
Moved apart across the bleak sky.

Lorna Rose Douglas (10)
St Peter's CE Primary School, East Bridgford

Scared

Trees sniggered in the cold whilst the leaves leapt
into the haunted house as the scared people
screamed in the darkness.

Rain crawled down the wet drainpipes like a person's blood dripping
from a surface as the scared people screamed in the darkness.

The windows grinned madly at me as the scared people
screamed in the darkness.

The haunted house turned into a face and I felt terrified
as the scared people screamed in the darkness.

Drawers banged in and out as the doors creaked as I opened them.
The scared peopled screamed in the darkness.

Chairs broke when I sat on them and the floorboards creaked
and I ran away!

Emma Hopewell-Ward (10)
St Peter's CE Primary School, East Bridgford

One Night . . .

Evil icicles sneered like cruel killers stalking the deadly night,

One night . . .
Crazy waterfalls screamed like crying children.

One night . . .
Scorching sun staggered across the dying sky,

One night . . .
Torn trees howled like lost babies.

One night . . .
Daggers of lightning crawled towards a forgotten world.

Alexandra Chick (11)
St Peter's CE Primary School, East Bridgford

Enchanted Horrors

A stone whistled as it skimmed the water,
And the screams of the ghosts got louder.
The roots crawled through the enchanted forest,
And the screams of the ghosts got louder.
All of the grass bowed to the grinning motor,
And the screams of the ghosts got louder,
The haunted house rattled,
And the screams of the ghosts got louder.
The deadly deafening howl as the coffin fell,
And the screams of the ghosts got louder.
Terror tree houses collapsed
And the screams of the dead got louder.
The clock shrieked as the deafening bell rang,
And the screams of the dead got louder.

I felt scared

And the screams of the ghosts died down.

Daniel Thurman (10)
St Peter's CE Primary School, East Bridgford

The Screams Of The Dead

The path twitched as the leaping leaves fell onto its muddy surface.

He ran as swift as the wind as the trees' gnarled knuckles
Reached out to take the scared struggling boy.

And the screams of the dead got louder.

The creepy mansion of madness laid down the wet muddy path
As the hand of the deer hunter enticed him in.

And the screams of the dead got louder.

The dark creepy house creaked as he walked up
The old rotten staircase the ghastly ghosts flew past
Like bats swooping and searching.

And the screams of the dead got louder.

The cold doors disintegrated as the floorboards broke
And the screams of the dead got louder.

The rotting walls crumbled as the ruined ceiling seeped water
And the screams of the dead got louder.

The long grass in the garden was colonised by gigantic
Whimpering worms and the screams of the dead got louder.

As the morning awoke the trees relaxed
And the screams of the dead died down.

Daniel Hayes (10)
St Peter's CE Primary School, East Bridgford

Water

The gush of water dawdled uncaringly by the
Rocks at the top of the white watered
Waterfall.
The shallow stream staggered along the
Stony cobbled riverbed.
The shallow water viciously shivered as a
Family of fish flung themselves up the
Waterfall.
The dam groaned as what seemed like
The whole sea piled up against it.
The river hesitated deeply as it cautiously
Entered the roaring sea.
The sea jolted as a shark attacked a
Helpless fish.
Ice cubes clung onto each other amongst
The huge waves of the Arctic.

Matthew Sutton (10)
St Peter's CE Primary School, East Bridgford

Hallowe'en

The moon shivered like a child frightened in
The mysterious midnight.
And the beat of the heart got louder.

A witch sniggered like a child keeping a
Secret in the silent scary night.
And the beat of the heart got louder.

The night swept like a curtain opening and
Closing showing the cold crashing dark sky.
And the beat of the heart got louder.

Shadows grabbed like a robber stealing
Jewellery sparkly, shiny gleams of gold.
And the beat of the heart got louder.

A wicked monster dawdled like an old man in
The misty moonlight.
And the beat of the heart got louder.

Vampires crept towards their coffins in the
Dark dusty night.
And the beat of the heart got louder.

All the clouds crawled away from the scary
Silent haunted house.
And the beat of the heart stopped!

Hannah Jayne Parker (10)
St Peter's CE Primary School, East Bridgford

One Night . . .

Bricks shivered like a cat purring angrily.
A tree screaming in the midnight moon reaching its bony fingers

onto you

The door melted like a cold tap dripping alone in the dark.
The rain grinned as if it was a witch out tonight.
The wind whispered in my cold ears while my teeth shook.
All the stars winked and woke the dead from their dull coffins.
An icicle pointed to a werewolf howling to the white moon.

Jessica Morrell (10)
St Peter's CE Primary School, East Bridgford

Scared

The huge sun danced elegantly like a beautiful
Ballerina winning the gold.
The silent, scared, shivering moon frowned like a
Deserted child.
The house stared into your eyes like a furious
Cheetah waiting to pounce.
A shadow mysteriously called her back like a weak,
Weary, middle-aged man.
A star staggered along the gigantic sky like a tiny
Fish lost in the ocean.
Lightning swayed slowly like a raindrop slipping
From a starry sky

And I was scared!

Brittany Howe (10)
St Peter's CE Primary School, East Bridgford

Scared!

The pumpkin grimaced as the scared children crept
Back into the mysterious midnight dark.
The moon hid behind the fluffy, ferocious, white
Clouds in the creepy blue sky.
The sun fell behind the horizon as the bright sky
Faded into the nervous night.
And I felt scared.

The waterfall sprinted past the deadly, dangerous rocks.
The tap drooled like a dead person lying helplessly on
The floor as blood trickled down his pale cheek.
And I felt scared.

Spiderwebs swung as the whispering wind breathed a heavy sigh.
Coffins thumped vigorously underground as the vicar droned on.
And I felt scared.

Katie Bailey (11)
St Peter's CE Primary School, East Bridgford

The Dark Night

The thunder and lightning squabbled like an old married couple.
Cold raindrops slowly drooled down the windowpane
like a waterfall on a grey misty morning.
A tree was flabbergasted as it was hit by lightning.
Doors wailed in the cold breeze
Pebbles heard the dangerous white foam of the waves crashing
on the shore.
The sun cowered behind the horizon
The dark green bush shuddered violently
Gloomy shadows grabbed dangerously
Grey ghastly ghosts whispered
When morning broke the zombies went back
to their creepy tombstones.

Dominic Wealthall (10)
St Peter's CE Primary School, East Bridgford

House Of Horrors

The sun shivered whilst it was shining
Through the clouds like lightning
It looked absolutely terrifying.

The thunder shouted to wake everyone up during
The night,
It sounded absolutely terrifying.
The shiny stars crawled along the lit up sky like a worn
out cloud,
It looked absolutely terrifying

The tall tree drooled down its old ratty trunk like an
Upset child,
It looked absolutely terrifying.
The flower creaked through its roots like a roaring
Tiger
It sounded absolutely terrifying.

Connor Prideaux (10)
St Peter's CE Primary School, East Bridgford

Untitled

Viciously the volcano dramatically drooled its lava,
Windows whined as they cracked in their frightening frames,
Screeching animals awoke the sleeping trees.

The luminous lightning vandalised the shuddering shaking building
Like a moaning monster,
Clouds creepily crept across the shivering sky.

Max Bradbury (10)
St Peter's CE Primary School, East Bridgford

Haunted Skeleton

The lightning bombed in the sky
The scream of the dead shattered the sky
A plane shot through the sky
The midnight moon stared like a silver blanket.
The bullet flew through the sky like a homing missile.

Thomas Orrey (10)
St Peter's CE Primary School, East Bridgford

Hallowe'en Horrors

Raindrops climbed down the slippery window.
The hailstones fell like a thousand
Knives cutting the earth,
The lake shivered as the wind came.
Leaves bounced from tree to tree.
The star grew bigger as the mist appeared.
The dead cigarette smoked a smiley grin.
Women screamed as their children were gone.
Owls howled as the lightning smacked the trees.

Poppy Whittington Devereux (10)
St Peter's CE Primary School, East Bridgford

My Journey Started When . . .

The old sun staggered after the moon trying
To reach out but failing every time.

The raging rain licked the sweaty soggy earth
Like a bloodthirsty vampire.

The collapsed clock clicked in anger,
Silently and suspiciously.

The jealous moss slithered up the tired wall.

The dark, dangerous, deathly, deadly sky
Frowned furiously and broke its
Promise for a brighter day.

The seaweed seemed to be holding back the
Roaring ripping raging sea as it backed
Away cautiously.

My journey ended when I saw a small
Helpless leaf falling in front of me it was
Swirling, whirling, grabbing, catching the
Freezing cold air.

Lydia Shacklock (10)
St Peter's CE Primary School, East Bridgford

I Was Petrified

The deserted mountain danced
Gracefully as the ice-cold snow
Slowly tickled its bony and spiny
Back like an avalanche storming
With fear.

The rocky wood beckoned the
Young girl like a wicked witch
Enticing a rat into her cauldron
She was petrified.

The moon waited silently and
Patiently like an everlasting rock
Waiting for the earth to pass by
And I felt petrified.

Heather Armstrong (10)
St Peter's CE Primary School, East Bridgford

One Scary Night . . .

Trees crept through the dark, creepy, muddy forest,
And the laugh of the vampire got louder.
The door creaked as loud as a giant amplifier,
And the laugh of the vampire got louder.
Lightning lit up the sky like a detonated bomb!
And the laugh of the vampire got louder.
The rain raced down the smashed window pane,
And the laugh of the vampire got louder.
The creepy pumpkin smiled like a mad clown,
And the laugh of the vampire got louder.

Joe Hughes (10)
St Peter's CE Primary School, East Bridgford